An offering

I0566917

WHO I WAS IS WHO I'LL NEVER BE

A POETIC INTRODUCTION

Emily-Rose

Who I Was is Who I'll Never Be

ISBN: 979-8-218-82149-4

TABLE OF CONTENTS

INTRODUCTION

I don't know how I got here. Though I am not quite sure where I am, I have never felt more at home. Navigating this world left me bare, the journey was long and unforgiving. I grew tired and stood at the peak with nothing left to lose. Suddenly the winds swept me away. I must have died and been reborn. Is this paradise? I didn't think I would make it. Is this a dream, or am I finally awakened?

LETTER TO THE DIVINE

So many times I lost my way,

Led astray by temporary pleasures and bad decisions

I believed the light you placed within me was enough to keep me from ruin

But you took everything

Lost and bare,

I laid in the ruins of myself with nothing left to offer but the silence of my soul

By giving me nothing, you gave me everything

Though surrounded by darkness, my faith in the light never wavered

I crawled through the darkness blindly,

Certain I would find you again

And there in the place I had once abandoned,

I met you once more

Not in triumph,

But in surrender

From the depths of the darkness you asked me to endure,

I have emerged.

No more blood on my hands

I garner my neck with garnet stones and gold,

To remember the bloodshed of my past

To defend against what may come for leaving it behind

I know they're watching me,

My enemies

But there will be no fresh blood on my hands no matter how they provoke me

Protected by Divine

The Gods keep them in line

Yet they wonder why they cannot touch me

DUALITY

I am the tower, I am the fool

I am the chaos, I am the healer

I am the damned, I am the holy

I am nothing if not everything all at once

THE MONSTER I AM

The fury in me is hard to subside

The rage I feel boils from my insides,

tempering me into a monstrous being

There was a time when I had no say

The transformation would take over me

But these days I hold the reins keeping the monster at bay

Though I have control,

She makes her presence known

Breathing down my neck

Lurking in the shadows of my mind telling me to come home

But I've abandoned that shelter long ago

The rage that lives inside me will never again be my home

I hold the reins

I have control

WHO I WAS IS WHO I'LL NEVER BE

Trust falling from the peak,

Forgetting all reality

Blindly falling into the tides and letting The Divine guide me

A rebirth from the ruins I left behind

A new world created just for me

Who I was is who I'll never be

ANOINTED

Humbled by the trials and darkness that consumed my mind

A place so far from the light that flowers couldn't grow

But through the cracks you shined as a glimmer of hope

In the darkness I crawled to you

And now I stand on my own

You knew my soul and you called me home

With the light of the heavens behind me,

I will never again be alone

Anointed by The Divine

It was only a matter of time

HOME IS WHERE THE HEART IS

I placed my heart in the hands of men who never truly saw me

With their greedy hands they stole all they could in an attempt to tarnish me

But from the ruins they would leave

I would rise again

Reclaiming what was mine,

Saving myself every time

I searched for home in fleeting arms but all along it was clear to see,

Home was always in me

So my heart will stay with me in a loving hold

Because despite their efforts to destroy me,

There is no tarnish born for gold

PARASITE

She cuts me until she draws blood to show me she
still has control

She stains my thoughts with filth to show the hold
she has over me

I can't turn away

There is no escape

She lives inside me

And her hunger runs deep

Only pain can satiate her

And she takes it in any form

Cutting me just enough to bleed

Piercing my heart with whispers of misery

She binds me to the cruel, the ones who echo her will

Each one a vessel to further her torment

She'll do anything for a taste,

Only drinking from the well of my pain

FINAL SCORE

Rushing to the end

Trying to find a good place to begin

Patience is a virtue

Or rather, a test

One that I continued to fail time and time again

Little did I know that everything I ever wanted was on the other side of a passing score

GNOSIS

The inner light that seeps from my soul is the lantern that illuminates my path

I find that in silence,

My knowledge comes in dreams and thoughts that pass

In my stillness The Divine guides my mind

PRISONER

A prisoner to a suit of flesh

What am I doing here?

Playing the role as well as I can without a script in my hand

A role I cannot quit,

A role I was forced to fit

Divine guides me in this life,

But did I ask for this?

The complexities of the human life live forefront in my mind

All I want to do is run and hide

Away from the emotions, away from the day to day

But there is no place on this stage where I won't be found

So I stand center stage and perform my role like a puppet on strings

When all is said and done

When the curtain is called

What will happen then?

Will I be forced to perform again?

THE TOWER

The tower collapsed everything I thought I knew

I rummaged through the ruins only to discover I
never had a clue

No idea of who I was or what I was to do

I sat in silence

And thus it spoke the truth as whispers guiding me
along

I followed the path

Every step bringing me closer to the dreams I'd
forgotten I had

A life I never imagined could be,

Built on the ruins of what needed to be released

Wheel of fortune

The wheel of fortune has turned in my favor

A long time coming,

But I had to pay my dues

My debt settled, fortune in my hands

I will not allow it to change who I am

With this new found luck my life has only just begun

What once only existed in my dreams is coming to fruition in reality

THE SACRED

REBELLION

THE PATH OF SELF DISCOVERY

AND

BECOMING THE MASTER OF YOUR

REALITY

———————

Emily-Rose

INTRODUCTION

The most rebellious thing we can do is go within ourselves and begin the journey of self-discovery. Stripping ourselves of everything we were told we needed to be in order to discover who we were created to be.

A rebellion that leads to the awakening of an undeniable truth, a truth that has been buried beneath layers of fear, shame and false narratives. An awakening that leads us not only to the core of who we are but also to the Divine light that exists within us. A rebellion to choose and defend the light despite being surrounded by darkness.

May your journey be full of wonder and reward.
It is never too late to begin again.

ABOUT AUTHOR

Emily-Rose is an introvert, a daydreamer, and a writer whose words often come to her in dreams. She has devoted her life to self-discovery; walking a path shaped by spirituality and solitude. Each story she writes is a step on her own journey shaped by vulnerability and the deep desire to learn who she truly is. Outside of writing, Emily-Rose is a passionate adventurer drawn to movement and art. Whether it's hiking remote trails, painting in her studio, or getting lost in her words, she's constantly chasing moments that ignite her creativity. Through her writing, Emily-Rose invites you to journey with her into erotic passion, self-discovery, and the truth that lingers in longing.